Undreaming Landscapes

Undreaming Landscapes

Poems by

Paula Friedman

Kelsay Books

Cover Art © 2015 Ian Parker
Titled "House on Fire"

ISBN 13: 978-0692486429

Kelsay Books
Aldrich Press
www.kelsaybooks.com
24600 Mountain Ave 35
Hemet, California 92544

In memory of my father

For my mother, Zoe, Eli

and for Pete

Acknowledgements:

Acknowledgements are made to the editors of the following publications in which some of these poems appeared.

Apple Press Review "Captured Mole"; *Blue Unicorn* "Cartoon Balloon"; *Columbia Journal of Art and Literature* "Undreaming Landscape"; *Michigan Quarterly Review* "Elegy For The Los Angeles River"; *Midwest Poetry Review* "Nightride"; *Prairie Schooner* "Possum Dream"; *Sequoia* "Moths"; *Main Street Rag* "Todos Santos"; *Birmingham Journal of Arts* "Waning June"; *Poetry Quarterly* "The Tellers"; *Southern Poetry Review* "Rusalki of the North"; *Cactus Heart Press* "A Daughter's Leavetaking"; *Kentucky Poetry Review* "Brother and Sister"; *Tikkun* "Commemoration."

Contents

Kelsay Books

Possum Dream

Always the same immobility–
black dome overhead
with a few cut-out stars,
and the moment, eternally expanding
until possum, road, headlights,
and the distanced sky
run seamlessly together
and there's no victim,
and the night's not
cold nor predatory.

This time the possum
unsticks itself, scuttles off
and vanishes in the shadows
while the car creeps on
keeping to first gear.
Everything remains
less final with us–nobody's killed off
and nobody gets away. I don't remember when
your mild gaze turned otherwise–a blade of light
simplified by will, honed thin,
but touching nothing.

My durability wears
as each new resolve
cracks and whittles itself
into complicity
until I'm all softness,
all receptivity.

It might as well be
a weapon, this way of
folding you in. At night
I dream of the possum,
its cloud-colored fur,
and scar-mouth unseaming
a slow unambiguous hiss.

Cartoon Balloon

Midday: sun striking roof
and tree. The spring crow
caws from the wire; I
enter the second season
of your leaving.

The garden in the yard
grows over: roots,
dead filaments; how
floridly the roses spill
their petals to the grass–
a million papery hearts.

Your face travels the air
like a cartoon balloon: it is
a messenger, mouthing out
thin inarticulate words; I am
no longer compelled to
make sense of it.

Stretched out warm under this
new April sun, I am content
to watch your small face float;
when I tire of it, the sky will
gape open like a mouth,
taking you in.

Elegy for the Los Angeles River

Dry, the heat could powder your bones
at noon while the sun's glare
magnifies each crack and flaw
in the concrete encasement.
The river's gone underground;
to keep us safe from floods,
the old watermen dammed it up.
Once willows leaned, following
its clean meanderings.
The world dies, then dies again.
I remember blown tumbleweeds
skittering into the bluish
autumn dusk, and oversize lizards,
eyes flicking, tail flicking as they
crept into our first floor rooms.
If the concrete were blasted open,
and the river let run,
would it spill from its
fixed channel into
a looser dance of youth,
and the drained,
brambly valley submerge?

They left no scenic openings
to flare into pools,
each rush sealed fast,
humanish as love
that's shoved down
below the skinline
and stricken with bitterness.

Wraith of old beauty
that belongs to us–
with river-shadow,
river-bone, streams
of car-colored steel
glinting in the near distance.

Salton Sea and Points West

Paradise eludes us, the good
dead provide no scrutable news
and so continue we must
in earthly evocation of
divinest places–heavenly
homes or homely havens
to house our restless waiting.
The question's the same:
where to from here?

Geography beckons us west
to jagged sea-salt edges, with
at least one desert to cross, or fix.
So much wavering dust-colored
dust, backed by magenta mountains
cannot be left untampered–
Even the bible tells us
that barrenness is waste.

Jury-rigged, hauled uphill, after
the rains the river blew its top,
spilled and spilled to overfill
a gritty saline basin. Vast,
silvery, dense with selenium,
a sudden sea appeared. With sleek
motels, pools, rows of imported palms,
a flim-flam fertility, not fit for farms
but maybe an American Riviera.

We're fast running out of
lapsed West. The real sea

can't serve as Paradise,
at least not one to house us long
without masks, fins, tanks of oxygen–
Or let an ancient stillness hold,
the centuries crumbling slowly on
as we flare accidental gills,
learn to breathe the salt.

Honey Island Swamp

Wintering, this swamp
looks more like a moonscape,
half sunk in a lunar river
breeding mist upon mist.
Even the alligators are submerged
in temporary mud-tombs;
their bog breath rises up,
breaking to bubbles on the water's surface
as if to say: "we're here; we're still here."

The beavers and nutrias
must be dozing further inland;
the mist obscures their shacks.
Twig-built, packed with grasses,
walled by nothing so thin
as a window, the shacks
are one of the last holdouts
against a soluble world.

Bald oaks, sweetgums, each
tree body barely pokes up,
having dwindled nearly to spirit.
The cold water (is it rising higher
up the boles?) is slick with duckweed,
and has turned a dead color.
This place reminds us of our own
deaths, always encroaching, but
not yet arriving -- the hearts of fish
ticking beneath the boat's bottom.

From Bora Bora

An island's not alone,
just look at the blue
Pacific lapping at its rim,
not to mention whole
boatloads of tourists
dying to get away
from larger chunks of land.
From anywhere faster,
more populous. The palms,
and their trim shadows give
a minimalist reassurance: life
will go more simply here.
At dusk, torchlight already
streaming across the water,
and the quay humming down,
it's hard to see the shoreline curve
back around itself, hard to see
your own reflection, single
or joined with another,
before restive waves
dive and divide it up.

Nightride

Because darkness transformed
the harsh
low-scrub hills and arena sands,
bleached white at noon,
into softer hues
of blues and browns,
it was possible to see
a sure gentleness in you,
as in the sweetly bold
not even green-broke colts
drowsing in the high pasture.
So we unstalled our horses
for the quiet thrill of a night ride.

We crossed the unlit road
stepping toward indigo hills
that sat indistinguishable
from the stretched tarpaulin sky.
Maybe you never felt peaceful –
with your tense, turned-in-on-themselves drawings,
neatly stacked in the dusty ranch trailer,
a revolver under your pillow.
Your boyish old cowboy clothes.
Whose dream were we that night? –
galloping into the stony open field,
doggedly clattering over that
uneven ground, as if there were
some measurable distance to cross,
sheer impulsion edging us on,
not towards one another, or anyone...

as if speed, darkness and the rapt
heat between us might
alter some larger thing–

Moths

I

First in Chicago, a child of five,
I watched them flutter for hours
round the small pale bulb
of my nightlight. Like me, I thought,
too restless for sleep. The summer nights
muggy and long as I listened
to my father wheeze in the next room.

II

The doctor said it would be
better in California; there my
father could breathe easily. No more
nights leaning into a fan to ease
the ugly asthmatic rasp he'd
picked up in the camp. Auschwitz:
a word I seldom heard but knew
it had something to do with
breathing. On the long drive,
I wondered if there would
be moths in California.

III

Moths flutter everywhere:
In Chicago, California,
in Ecuador, Peru and Bolivia.
In a one-room hut in Coroico,
delicate white moths,
nervy and quick with energy,

winged round the flames of candles.
Restless as ever I watched them, imagining
my father's wheeze in the next room.

Still in Coroico, I dreamed of an Indian.
In a strange tongue he told me
moths were white magic; kept close
to the body they insured immortality.
He opened his robe and out flew
a swarm of white moths.
With a smile and a sweep of his hand
he gathered them back.

IV

For years I forgot about moths.
Less restless at night, I no longer
watched them. The doctor in Chicago
was right: most nights my father
breathes easily. But last night
moths returned to me in dream:
walking with my father
through the greenest of fields,
the high grass rolled toward us
like sea-waves. We were dressed
in white robes, moths
fluttered against our breasts.
At the field's end, was a gate
with a name painted on it;
the word seemed familiar,
but I couldn't pronounce it.

Inside, hordes of people
milled naked, hands covering
themselves with shame.
Many opened their mouths
as if wishing to scream:
white soundless moths
flew out of them. The crowd
pressed us back; now moths
were everywhere.

V

Tonight flames leap and brighten.
White importunate moths
flutter against the window pane,
wishing to be let in. Snuffing
out the fire I watch them
scatter and recede like hard stars
into the long changeless night.

Commemoration

We don't name our children for the living,
as if the named-for might
hurry the first to his end.
We commemorate losses instead.
My son's named for an uncle
I've never seen. My father says his
brother was a shy, silent man; in 44
,he went up in a shaft of smoke.
And I have this uneasiness
as if maybe our renaming is
tinged with morbidity; or worse,
that the Hebraic names themselves,
Eli, Rachael, Sarah, Chaim,
might reconjure history: first the
oddly still villages and burnt fields–

When my father looks at my daughter
he sees his niece: a four-year-old
with goldish, hay-colored hair.
Then he tells a story (over and again):
It was winter, snow was everywhere,
the night was cold, sharp as ice.
Rachael walked close to her mother,
arm in arm, as their line swerved,
no, sharply branched to the left,
trees, tree-shadow obscuring them all.
Each time he tells it, I try to see her
more clearly (what is it I hope to see?).
She might have turned for a moment,
maybe waved and called to the others,
then quickened her step
like any child with somewhere to go.

The Tellers

Blameless as rain
the children were given
sweet parts. In the chill thinning
sun they haunt the lawns
hunting rich mulch for
winter blossoms, ghost bones,
anything delicate or strange.
When the sun slips down
they lean toward our voices,
the lit house taking them in.

Tonight grandpa will arrive,
and the kids will clamor for stories
heard a dozen times before:
camels trekking across white sand;
Europe's nobility honoring him with
numbers tattooed above his wrist–

We know these stories cannot last,
that soon whimsy will give way to fact.

Why should they come in at all?
Leave them browsing in the
blue dusk, their small frames
bending wordlessly over each
grave of leaves, beyond reach.

Brother and Sister

Red brick and snow,
that's what I remember of Chicago.
And always with me,
maybe too much with me,
my brother, my guardian.
He showed me the windows locked
too tight to let in Tony the bum
our backalley phantom.
Taught me how to walk on ice
without falling. In the street,
courtyard, he watched me,
watched me well until
we had no separate lives.

But all the while,
from somewhere out of sight,
another, no, two other
stories grew, and stuck:
I turned witch who
ate his boyhood up,
and he the wolf,
who one by one,
blew my houses down.
It's been years now,
but sometimes in half dream
I see my room fill up with snow,
and we're back again
on Thome Street slope,
our sled skidding out
from under us, both of us
falling, and separate.

Captured Mole

Something the cats dragged in,
rattling in the moonless black,
a sound more machinelike
than creaturely. Just a mole,
clicking and quivering, but
unmaimed yet, no thanks to
the pointy racks of feline teeth.

The prowling robust boys
dumped their prize, scuttled off
as my chicken scream split up the darkness,
hands fumbling for light. Slick-furred,
blunt-nosed and motionless, there
it was, alone under a blaring bulb.
Why should a little wildness
lugged inside unnerve me so?

I imagine it too terrifying
to be whisked up from the dank
wooded yard, the dense,
tangled ivy, and rooty cypress,
transported in the blink
of shrewder eyes to this strange
nether world, now pitilessly lit,
without even the smell of earth.

Undreaming Landscape

Hot winds lashing overwires,
sky a-skitter with crisp
maple leaves, and sirens.
My mind weds each to each
as if wild prophecy
blows in from without.
Out here, thinner bones
meld with the sunset
and darkness only consoles
a blackout heart.
Before my eyes, the sun
cedes to a brightness;
in blue air the atom splits–
Nothing pictures it, not
wires, sirens, the refracting sky,
nor these maples buckling
close as hidden children.

Rusalki of the South

Rusalki are the waternymphs of Slavic myth.

We are drowned girls, they say:
once we walked upright, alone

or coupled in the verdant woods,
alongside the cold Danube,

purposeful in the world until
sudden grief or accident

funneled us under. But
fluidity has its perfections,

bending the gross light
into a panoply of color,

and the weightlessness,
the sheer relief of it! Arms,

legs, face – my face – lifted
with so little gravity, the other

maidens attending me, and I
them, all in shimmering robes,

luminous as infant skin.
Still we wish to be counted

among the undead,
mercifully remembering

no other life but this—
sealed-off chilly languor

and our delicate singing to bewitch
or console others with our fate.

Rusalki of the North

Down here, the wan light
increases our skin's pallor
and they say our lean bodies
look cadaverous. But why should
we mind what the living say?

Unlike our southern sisters,
we have accepted our fate
without hope or pretence.
I, for one, was not lured here
by any dazzling, sleight-of-hand

watery sprite. Stones dragging
my apron bottom, I entered
the chill Danube free of will.
Its icy waters soothed my flaming
heart. Betrayed by Uri, my prince

of a man, who cruelly eclipsed me
with a mere child, no lovelier than I.
Now a green fire lights our eyes
and our hair spills ragged,
tangly as willow roots.

Watching the young, drunk
on love, strolling the waters' edge,
deaf to the moon's blackening
cackles, blind to our
slippery moss-gloved hands

and cruder nakedness
beneath the surface scrim,
we remember such oblivion–
knowing neither how deep
the river bottom, nor how cold.

Rusalki on the Loose

I cannot stay put–
the tepid south too slow
with its maidens' traipsing melodies
and my lips upturned
in a firm scar of a smile.

I remember the slip,
my knees and shins scraping
the rivers' cobbled edge.
Try as I did, I could not
learn to bewitch, lured

no sylvan maidens down
with fluttery song.
The others regarded me
as foolish, an obstinate,
void of promise.

When bolder sprites
busted open the dikes--
grey stone crumbling
from grey stone--,
freeing the river's flow,

I fled north, way up
to the taigan lakes where
bitch-hags swarm, their
drained pallorous faces
surfacing only at night.

Dead-souled, stone-cold
from nipple to crotch,
they'd take anyone in.
I couldn't match them,
unable to coax lover,
sister or stranger down.

Shame roils up and warms me
as, back and forth, I swim
in a cloudy interim, eluding
the coarse rigor mortis
of despair, and hope, also.

Catteleyas

I hover over them like a nurse
with my tub of *Bloom-it,*
misting, adjusting their positions,
trying to light on the one right fix.
Catteleyas need brightness, a western view.
Still mine are bloomless. Maidenhair
ferns too are difficult, their intricate
stitchwork so quick to shrivel.
Their failure to thrive is expected,
though always a disappointment.
I should switch to heartier things–
striped spider plants, a twilled cactus. . .

Last year the Catteleyas were majestic;
fresh from the nursery, their velvet
petal bursts startling as new love.
And then the crushing lapses
(too little water, too much light?),
as when the man slowly retreats
into his distances, and the woman
tallies their limitations, exactly.
Inch by inch, row by row. . .
how does that cheerful child's song go?
Neither of us remembers now
when the deep pink buds were
glowing and opening
in Paradise.

Morning

Up through cloudfall and calm bay,
the sun rises so prettily—
How I hate morning, each day
opening like a wound, demanding
such stoic composure, presence.

The pale brightness hurts my eyes
and reminds me you still exist,
unfathomably separate, occupying
your own time and space. It is
an accomplishment, I suppose,
to step out of the known world.

We who are left lack
capacity for such grand gesture.
One foot planted on each side of
a border that pitilessly divides
then and now, we look on, skeptical
wary of another future.

We grow impatient for night,
its dark reprieve from so many
exacting performances; then you
grow less real. We forget you—
mere shadow of a man.
You wane and thin to no one.

Waning June

Remember when summer spelled giddy reprieve—
the valley's white heat relieved
by rivers, lakes, the inexhaustible sea,
and the precise point at which it appeared
to meet the wide sky's edge, the horizon distant
enough to quell your fear of endings.

How did you arrive at this moment, the trail
behind littered with lost or discarded loves,
inhospitable houses, vacancies, and your own
willful inhospitalities? Even your children
no longer belong here; they are breathing
in their own difficult seasons.

During these waning summer nights
you attempt to remember, calculate, over
and again, what gifts you have given them,
what injuries. Listen: mathematics cannot
help you. There is no sum to these parts.

Possum Crossing

This is the time of night
when the engines thin
melding with the wind
in the criss-cross pines
while a saluki's bark sharpens.
Trees, and their shadows,
weave a tunnel through which
the curved road passes,
then disappears. Before
that last lit bend a possum
is scuttling. Hunched,
elderly, unbothered by me,
she keeps a steady trek
as if familiar with these parts.
Under the lamp, her
cloudy fur looks a bit
worse for wear–notched
and matted at the back.

How long do possums live?
How little I know about them!
Shy, myopic, they appear
most often at night,
looking more like giant rats
than like themselves.

In bold daylight once
we found a plush-furred infant,
stunned, at the road's edge–
sheer air surrounding her.
We lightly prodded, urging
her back into a deeper thicket.

By dusk she'd vanished, leaving us
to wonder if she'd found her kin.
Maybe she's grown now
into the raggedy-coated veteran
making her nightly pilgrimage
down to the lower woods.

Northwest Wildlife says
that despite their timidity,
possums can be fierce–
boldly smuggling themselves
into basements, sheds, then
settling in, cozily at home.

Cozy as we are each year
in our summer rentals–
the briny drift and damp
moldering tiles sending
us back and back
to all the years before.

Did we never leave? Has
the place been ours all along?
The owners safely out of view,
maybe inland for the season,
letting themselves go, like us,
mildly amnesiac, mis-remembering

who we meant to be (creatures solidly
at ease, in place…). At home, scrambling
for misplaced keys, eye glasses, phones,
we might step into the basement
and find moonlight pooling in pale fur,
(suddenly we're the intruders!),

as a possum rears up on,
bony haunches, startlingly lean
beneath a dense twill coat–
squinching its tight black eyes,
and hissing and hissing
the ancient night away.

A Daughter's Leavetaking

I saw no foreshadowing,
nor could I have imagined
this colder more distant orbit
when as a child of four or five
she slipped outside the cabin door
on a night lit by the thinnest moon.
High unstable drifts surrounded her–
small face rapt as if gripped in trance.
I watched her child body take off,
whirling and whirling
alone in the ghostly snow.

At Joshua Tree

Spareness clears the mind–
sand stretching far as the mountains
with sandstone formations
and spiky-limbed Joshua trees
beneath scant cloud-shred.
Nothing looks overdone.
Mentored by a landscape
both open and shy, we
shed what's unnecessary.

Those of us who confess
we love the desert best
must be a leaner lot than most,
embarrassed by effusion–the dense
profusion of colorful blooms–
as if abundant brilliance betrayed
beauty too easily achieved.

It's come to seem ritual,
cleansing, this pilgrimage.
On blazing afternoons we practice
walking through solid air,
heat-dreamy, we imagine ourselves
old, nomadic souls, not
balking at what's arduous,
nor agitated by emptiness.
Starting all over again.

Todos Santos

Lingering on the tiled patio,
we sit face to face under steady skies
all new, all blue silhouetting
stony saints and mountain-tops.

Down here, the close sun dissolves
our prickly wariness, obscures
the past, those self-built
ruins we prefer calling Fate.
I try to picture our faces
as somebody else might see them–
silly grins, twin mirrors
shining with something like love

or enchantment. Who can say? Surely
the night will wholly enfold us, its
benign breeze shuddering leaves, petals
pressing lip to lip in the darkness.

Respite

Call it summer then,
air thick and motionless,
framing the poppies' flicker
against close, burnished hills,
while, heat-soothed for the moment,
I am all me again, held in
place by such palpable light.
Good riddance to the stiff bone chill
and dawn's frosty lacework
softening to fog until
the wind, jumpy as nerves,
disperses it. I do not wish
to banish the seasons, but
let them linger elsewhere,
save summer with its opulent
kindness, in which I too can
don high color, brightness with less notice,
as day after light-shot day,
I may pose and glow.

Bunchgrass

On our familiar walks
through the neighborhood,
admiring its scattery, variegated gardens
thick with bunchgrass, cactus,
slabs of flaming granite–

the week's injuries rise
settling round our heads like
cold clouds. Always, I want
hushed the vague, glib apologies
while you insist

my bovine ruminations
quit. Back and forth,
the weather shifts between us
until suddenly, the high winds fall
with unexpected gentleness.

Then, without knowing why,
or exactly when, we go hand
in hand again, circling back
toward home, wordlessly content

to leave the day unfinished.

About the Author

Paula Friedman was born in Chicago but has spent most of her life living in various parts of California. She has worked as a freelance reviewer for many of the nation's major newspapers, including *The New York Times*, *The Washington Post* and *The Chicago Tribune*, to name a few, as well as for literary reviews including *The New Criterion* and *The Boston Literary Review*. Her poems have appeared in *Prairie Schooner*, *The Michigan Quarterly Review*, *The Southern Poetry Review* and others. She teaches writing and literature at California College of the Arts and Saint Mary's College in Moraga.

Made in the USA
San Bernardino, CA
20 September 2015